Marketing with Mini-Talks
& Mini-Books Made Easy

How to Powerfully Position Yourself as a
Speaker & Author with Less Effort
(Creation Planner)

Alicia "WATERS"

**Marketing with Mini-Talks & Mini-Books
Made Easy**

For ordering, booking, permission, or questions, contact the author.
www.amazon.com/author/alicianwaters
www.anwempires@gmail.com

ISBN-13:978-1721882779

Printed in the United States of America by Create Space

Marketing with Mini-Talks & Mini-Books Made Easy

Powerfully Position Yourself as a Speaker & Author with Less Effort

In the emerging new era of speakers and authors, most are realizing that using speaking and publishing as a marketing component isn't an option. Both of these areas are really starting to work together like a hand and glove. The model for effective outreach and impact is the speak to market path.

Every time leaders or entrepreneurs speak, it is a form of marketing. Speaking is considered the new marketing. Actually, this isn't a new concept; however, several are becoming more conscious of this evolving truth and its effectiveness.

Your marketing model should consist of not just your social media platforms of posting ads and promos consistently or randomly, your marketing model should consist of you speaking as a marketing strategy even if it's in mini-talk format.

One of the best ways to maximize your marketing and powerfully position your success with less effort is by creating 5 to 15 minute mini-talks as lead-ins to bigger talks and 30 to 70 page 5x8 mini-books as lead magnets to leverage your time and

Marketing with Mini-Talks & Mini-Books Made Easy

resources in order to make a true connection with your ideal audience.

So, if you're over the extensive hustle and grinding of marketing your works and still seeing little to no real results, a great and simple way to start is by using or repurposing online media platforms like, Blogtalkradio,YouTube, Soundcloud, Spreaker and/or even conference lines in a new way to up-level your marketing approach as a speaker by doing short, yet powerful segments that serve a mini-talks.

Another great method for mini-talks is having a short elevator pitch style of communication, using motivational coaching moments and/or a two to seven minute conversational style keynote even if you're only sharing with someone you see on the street or randomly come across in a grocery store who might be interested in what you do. This can also lead into sharing your mini-book for either purchase and/or leaving one with them as a way of reconnecting.

As it relates to the publishing aspect, whether you're creating a mini-book as a beefed-up business card to share about your products and service or promote a smaller version of a bigger book project that you're working on to provide as an introduction, adding a mini-talk in the form of an mp3, radio interviews clips or 30 seconds to two minute sound-bites will help you discover that the simple creation, marketing, and cash flow process for this endeavor is well worth it.

Amazon's print-on-demand company known as Createspace provides a DIY service for individuals to become self-published and you don't even need a budget to do so. Visit www.createspace.com and sign up for a free account and follow their easy set-up process for getting started.

Again, if you're tired of the constant hustle and grind of marketing and/or desire to take things to the next level, here are a few benefits and tips to help you jump-start your success with mini-talks and self-publishing mini-books that will maximize your marketing efforts.

Benefits of Creating a Mini-Talks & 5x8 Mini-Book for Marketing that Helps You to Maximize Your Marketing

* It saves on your time for broadcasting or recording speaking products. It's great for leveraging time for writing and self-publishing by producing a modest amount of content.

* It helps to expand your marketing budget and allows you to save on spending money for unnecessary marketing materials and tools.

Marketing with Mini-Talks & Mini-Books Made Easy

* It strengthens your ability to leverage and position yourself in the marketplace as a credible expert by having a speaking product, communications platform and a published book of some sort.

Tips for How Mini-Talks & Mini-Books Can Work Together Like a Hand & Glove

* **Speak Your Book:** Recording a five to ten minute presentation or TED-Talk format whether by way of radio, video or television about your mini-book can help to connect you with your audience as an introduction to your platform or update current followers for new launches or other endeavors.

* **Showcase as a Promotional Combo:** Craft an email to media outlets and/or speakers bureaus and send them an mp3 sample, radio interview, television feature or a short video presentation along with an attachment of your pdf or Kindle version of your mini-book.

* **Express Your Message Through a Live or Virtual Event:** You could create a teleseminar, webinar, book-signing party or small conference to provide a 15 to 30 minute mini-message that's crafted from your books primary intent. You could host an hour of networking or making strong connection with your tribe and/or colleagues and create a mini-talk and burn it to CD's to complement your mini-book to either give out or sell.

Marketing with Mini-Talks & Mini-Books Made Easy

There are levels of infinite possibilities with using this method for marketing to help you maximize your success. Use this creation planner to help you design your success formula for using mini-talks and mini-books to powerfully position your speaker's and/or author's platform.

Rinse and repeat this process and often as needed to ensure continued success.

Marketing with Mini-Talks & Mini-Books Creation Planning Section

Mini-Talks & Mini-Books Marketing Creation Planning

Record your reflections, insights and thoughts from the readings to create your mini-talks, write your mini-book projects and/or craft your marketing plan.

More Notes:

Mini-Talks & Mini-Books Marketing Creation Planning

Record your reflections, insights and thoughts from the readings to create your mini-talks, write your mini-book projects and/or craft your marketing plan.

Marketing with Mini-Talks & Mini-Books Made Easy

More Notes:

Mini-Talks & Mini-Books Marketing Creation Planning

Record your reflections, insights and thoughts from the readings to create your mini-talks, write your mini-book projects and/or craft your marketing plan.

More Notes:

Mini-Talks & Mini-Books Marketing Creation Planning

Record your reflections, insights and thoughts from the readings to create your mini-talks, write your mini-book projects and/or craft your marketing plan.

More Notes:

Mini-Talks & Mini-Books Marketing Creation Planning

Record your reflections, insights and thoughts from the readings to create your mini-talks, write your mini-book projects and/or craft your marketing plan.

More Notes:

Mini-Talks & Mini-Books Marketing Creation Planning

Record your reflections, insights and thoughts from the readings to create your mini-talks, write your mini-book projects and/or craft your marketing plan.

More Notes:

Mini-Talks & Mini-Books Marketing Creation Planning

Record your reflections, insights and thoughts from the readings to create your mini-talks, write your mini-book projects and/or craft your marketing plan.

More Notes:

Mini-Talks & Mini-Books Marketing Creation Planning

Record your reflections, insights and thoughts from the readings to create your mini-talks, write your mini-book projects and/or craft your marketing plan.

More Notes:

Mini-Talks & Mini-Books Marketing Creation Planning

Record your reflections, insights and thoughts from the readings to create your mini-talks, write your mini-book projects and/or craft your marketing plan.

More Notes:

Mini-Talks & Mini-Books Marketing Creation Planning

Record your reflections, insights and thoughts from the readings to create your mini-talks, write your mini-book projects and/or craft your marketing plan.

Marketing with Mini-Talks & Mini-Books Made Easy

More Notes:

Mini-Talks & Mini-Books Marketing Creation Planning

Record your reflections, insights and thoughts from the readings to create your mini-talks, write your mini-book projects and/or craft your marketing plan.

Marketing with Mini-Talks & Mini-Books Made Easy

More Notes:

Mini-Talks & Mini-Books Marketing Creation Planning

Record your reflections, insights and thoughts from the readings to create your mini-talks, write your mini-book projects and/or craft your marketing plan.

More Notes:

Mini-Talks & Mini-Books Marketing Creation Planning

Record your reflections, insights and thoughts from the readings to create your mini-talks, write your mini-book projects and/or craft your marketing plan.

More Notes:

Mini-Talks & Mini-Books Marketing Creation Planning

Record your reflections, insights and thoughts from the readings to create your mini-talks, write your mini-book projects and/or craft your marketing plan.

Marketing with Mini-Talks & Mini-Books Made Easy

More Notes:

Mini-Talks & Mini-Books Marketing Creation Planning

Record your reflections, insights and thoughts from the readings to create your mini-talks, write your mini-book projects and/or craft your marketing plan.

Marketing with Mini-Talks & Mini-Books Made Easy

More Notes:

Mini-Talks & Mini-Books Marketing Creation Planning

Record your reflections, insights and thoughts from the readings to create your mini-talks, write your mini-book projects and/or craft your marketing plan.

More Notes:

Mini-Talks & Mini-Books Marketing Creation Planning

Record your reflections, insights and thoughts from the readings to create your mini-talks, write your mini-book projects and/or craft your marketing plan.

More Notes:

Mini-Talks & Mini-Books Marketing Creation Planning

Record your reflections, insights and thoughts from the readings to create your mini-talks, write your mini-book projects and/or craft your marketing plan.

More Notes:

Mini-Talks & Mini-Books Marketing Creation Planning

Record your reflections, insights and thoughts from the readings to create your mini-talks, write your mini-book projects and/or craft your marketing plan.

More Notes:

Mini-Talks & Mini-Books Marketing Creation Planning

Record your reflections, insights and thoughts from the readings to create your mini-talks, write your mini-book projects and/or craft your marketing plan.

Marketing with Mini-Talks & Mini-Books Made Easy

More Notes:

Mini-Talks & Mini-Books Marketing Creation Planning

Record your reflections, insights and thoughts from the readings to create your mini-talks, write your mini-book projects and/or craft your marketing plan.

More Notes:

Mini-Talks & Mini-Books Marketing Creation Planning

Record your reflections, insights and thoughts from the readings to create your mini-talks, write your mini-book projects and/or craft your marketing plan.

More Notes:

Mini-Talks & Mini-Books Marketing Creation Planning

Record your reflections, insights and thoughts from the readings to create your mini-talks, write your mini-book projects and/or craft your marketing plan.

More Notes:

Mini-Talks & Mini-Books Marketing Creation Planning

Record your reflections, insights and thoughts from the readings to create your mini-talks, write your mini-book projects and/or craft your marketing plan.

Marketing with Mini-Talks & Mini-Books Made Easy

More Notes:

More Notes:

Write a brief summary about your mini-talks and mini-books marketing creation planning experience.

Summary Continued:

Marketing with Mini-Talks & Mini-Books
Made Easy

For More Resources

www.marketingwith5x8minibooks.tumblr.com

www.amazon.com/author/alicianwaters
Or
To Book the Author
For Speaking Engagements

Email: www.anwempires@gmail.com

If you enjoyed this resource, please consider writing a review on Amazon.com

Thanks & Blessings!

Marketing with Mini-Talks & Mini-Books Made Easy